CONTENTS

WHAT YOU NEED

The crafts in this book use materials that you can find in art shops, stationers and around your home. This page shows you the materials you will need to make lots of craft ideas.

Glue stick

Pencils

Marker pens

PVA glue

Scissors

Tape

Coloured paper and thin card

Paper fasteners

Follow the simple step-by-step guides to create these wonderful results! Find out how to make hissing snakes, rocking robots and much more.

LET'S GET STARTED!

BOBBY the fish

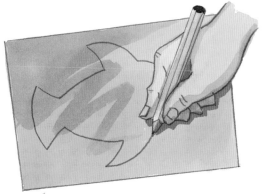

1 Draw out a simple shape for Bobby on thin card.

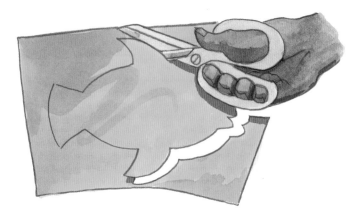

2 Carefully cut around it with scissors.

3 Cut out Bobby's body shape in a different colour paper.

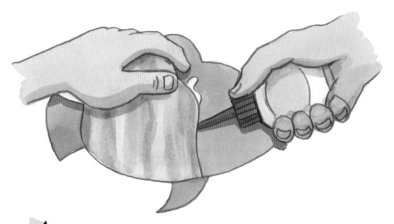

4 Glue it onto the body.

5 Cut out a small circle. Using a marker pen, draw on the eye. Glue down.

You could make lots of different fish designs – try using stripes or shiny foil!

Gulp!

Gulp!

Gulp!

7

STAINED GLASS WINDOW

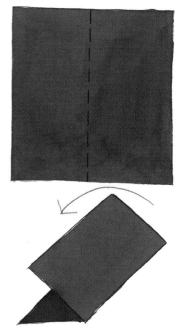

1 Fold a piece of paper in half.

2 Cut out a window frame (as shown).

3 Unfold the paper. Glue a strip of paper to the middle of the window frame.

4 Take another piece of paper and cut out the same sized window shape again.

8

5 Cut out different shapes of coloured paper.

6 Glue these onto your second window shape to make a collage.

7 Glue the collage behind the window frame.

9

SIMON
the snake
Hiss!

Hiss!

1 Make a small stack of different coloured pieces of paper (as shown).

2 Cut them into small strips.

3 Glue these strips onto a sheet of paper (as shown). This is Simon the snake's body.

4 Cut out his head shape from a piece of thin card.

Hiss!

Hiss!

5 Cut paper shapes for Simon's eyes and tongue and glue onto the face. Draw in his nostrils using a marker pen.

11

JIM & JOHN
the jellyfish

1 Cut a paper plate in half to make Jim and John.

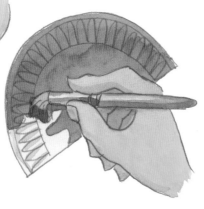

2 Now paint each half a different colour.

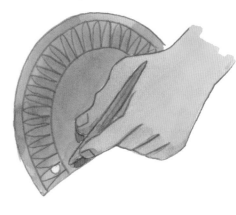

3 Make holes along the flat edges. Ask an adult to help.

4 Cut out paper eyes. Glue on and add dots with a marker pen.

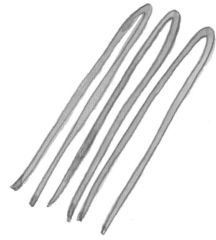

5 Find some pieces of string or wool.

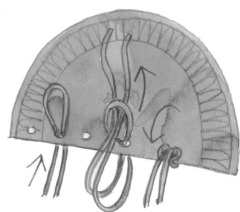

6 Pull the string through the holes and knot it (as shown).

Wobble!
Wobble!

ALBERT
the owl

Hoot!
Hoot!

1 Cut an owl-shaped body from a piece of thin card.

2 Glue on two paper circles for Albert's eyes.

3 Add dots to the eyes. Cut a piece of paper. Draw in feather shapes and glue on.

4 Cut out Albert's wings and beak from thin card. Glue on.

5 Stick Albert the owl onto a piece of coloured card. Draw and paint in a branch.

6 Cut out two paper shapes for Albert's feet and glue on (as shown).

Hoot!

Hoot!

Hoot!

15

OSCAR
the penguin

1 Cut out and stick down the shape of a chunk of ice. Now add a wavy shape below.

2 Cut out Oscar's orange feet from paper. Stick down.

3 Cut out and add Oscar's body and head shapes.

4 Now add his wings and white tummy.

5 Cut and glue on his eyes and beak. Add dots.

16

BARNEY the turtle

1 Fold a paper plate in half and cut it.

2 Paint it green. Leave to dry.

3 Paint a pattern on Barney's shell.

Swim!

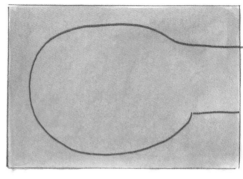

4 Cut out shapes for Barney's flippers and tail from a piece of thin green card. Paint on coloured dots.

5 Now draw the shape of his head onto the green card.

5 Now draw the shape of his head onto the green card.

6 Cut out and draw Barney's eyes and mouth (as shown).

Swim!

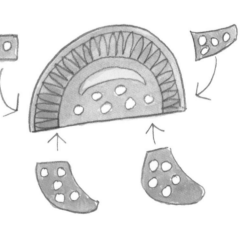

7 Glue Barney's head, flippers and tail onto his body.

19

JESS
the bee

1 Draw the wing shapes on a piece of thin card. Cut out.

2 Cut out an oval body shape from different coloured thin card.

3 Glue the body shape onto the wings.

4 Stick onto a sheet of paper. Draw in Jess' face, stripes, antennae and legs.

Buzz!

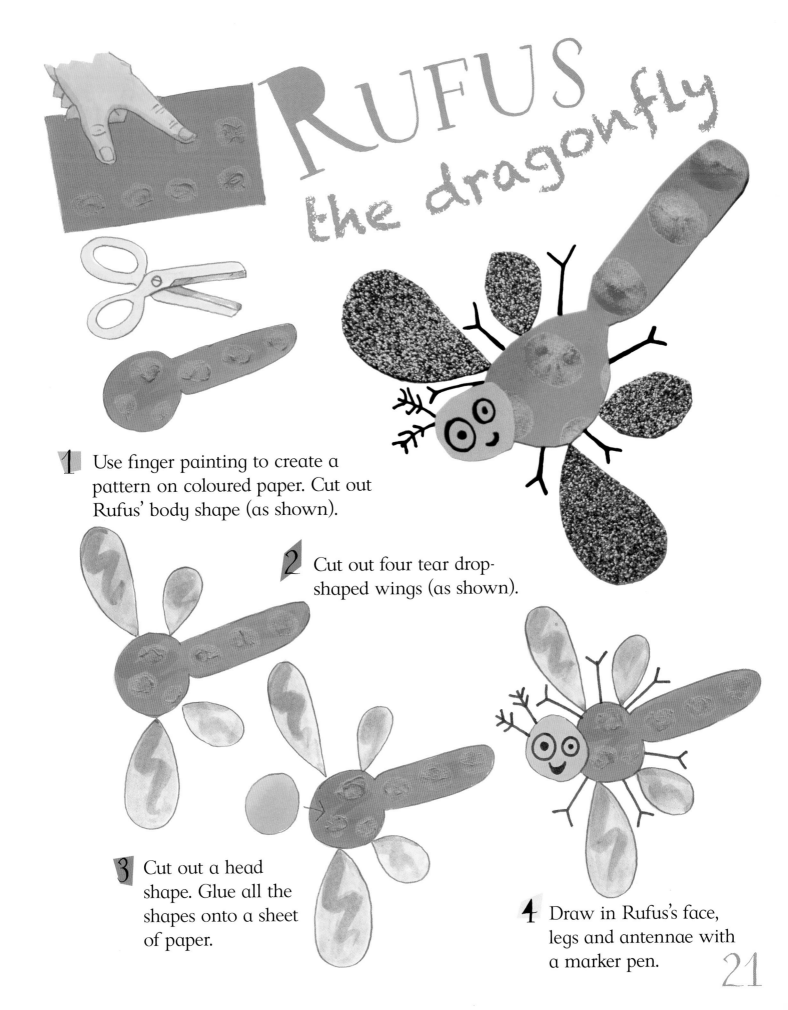

RUFUS the dragonfly

1 Use finger painting to create a pattern on coloured paper. Cut out Rufus' body shape (as shown).

2 Cut out four tear drop-shaped wings (as shown).

3 Cut out a head shape. Glue all the shapes onto a sheet of paper.

4 Draw in Rufus's face, legs and antennae with a marker pen.

21

DIANA the dragon

Roar!

Roar!

1 Draw in a dragon-shaped body and tail on a piece of thin card.

2 Cut out shapes for the head, wings and legs (as shown).

3 Make holes and use paper fasteners to join all the parts together. (Ask an adult to help.)

22

4 Now draw in Diana's eye and nostril. Cut out jagged-shaped teeth (as shown).

5 Cut out orange paper flames. Glue onto her mouth and add teeth.

Roar!

Roar!

23

COLLAGE
monsters

FINGER PAINTED SPLODGES

1

Cut out the shapes for
your monster's body,
arms and legs from
pieces of thin card.

Roar!

2 Cut out a jagged shape
for the monster's hair.
Experiment with different
hairstyles for each monster.

3 Cut and glue on the monster's claws.

4 Cut out and glue on your monster's jagged teeth and hair.

5 Cut out and glue on your monster's eyes. Add dots.

Growl!

Grrrr!

25

DORA
the driver

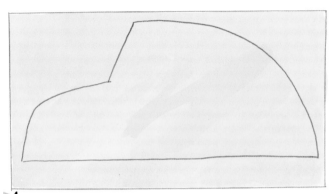

1 Draw a simple car shape on a piece of thin card. Cut it out.

2 Cut out window shapes from thin blue card. Draw in Dora.

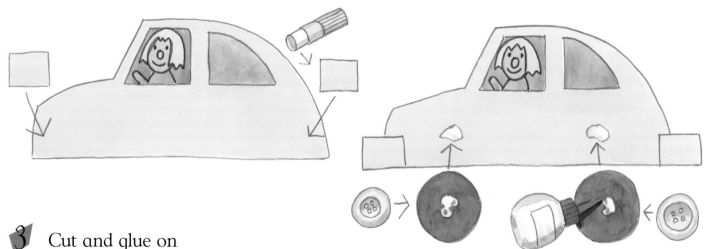

3 Cut and glue on shapes for the front and back bumpers. Add the windows.

4 Cut circles from thin black card for wheels. Glue a button to the middle of each and add to the car.

5 Cut out the shape of the surf board, the flowers and the light.

Vrooom! Vrooom!

6 Stick the surf board, the flower shapes and lights onto Dora's car.

27

ROLAND the robot

1

Cut an oval shape from a thin piece of textured blue card.

2

Cut and add small rectangles of card for Roland's arms and legs.

3

Cut out and add his hands and feet.

4

Cut out and add Roland's neck and head.

5

Cut out and add his ears. Draw in Roland's facial features.

6

Add more details to his body using a marker pen.

28

7 See how many different types of robot you can create.

Bleep!

Bloop!

Beep!

SPOOKY COLLAGE

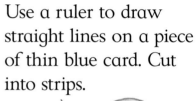

1 Use a ruler to draw straight lines on a piece of thin blue card. Cut into strips.

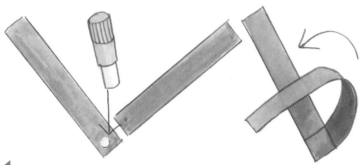

2 Glue two of the strips together (as shown).

3 Fold one strip over on top of the other.

4 Keep folding each strip in turn until it forms an accordion shape.

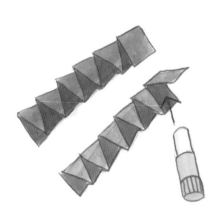

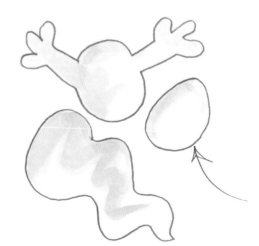

5 Add glue to the end of one accordion shape.

6 Cut out shapes for the ghost's head, body and tail from thin white card.

7 Draw a face on the ghost's head.

8 Glue this accordion strip onto the ghost's tail.

9 Glue the body shape to the other end of the strip.

10 Now join the body and head using the other accordion strip.

Wooooo!

Wooooo!

31

GLOSSARY

Bumpers horizontal bars on the back and front of a car, designed to help reduce damage in a car crash.

Flippers broad, flat limbs some animals have, allowing them to move quickly through water.

Ghost the restless spirit of someone who has died.

Marker pen a type of pen that makes bold, wide lines.

Paper fastener a piece of stationery used to hold separate pieces of paper together.

Shell a hard case some animals, like turtles, have to protect themselves.

Stained glass window windows containing coloured glass, often found in churches.

Surfboard a smooth wooden board used to ride, or surf, on waves.

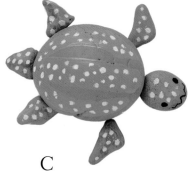

INDEX